THE SITUATION & WHAT CROSSES IT

THE SITUATION & WHAT CROSSES IT

Amy Schrader

Poetry
ISBN 978-1-936657-12-4

Cover photo: Jamie Wilson

Author photo: Jamie Wilson

Book design by Tonya Namura
using Gentium Basic

MoonPath Press is dedicated to publishing the
best poets of the U.S. Northwest Pacific states

MoonPath Press
PO Box 1808
Kingston, WA 98346

MoonPathPress@yahoo.com

http://MoonPathPress.com

for Chris
(Page of Cups)

ACKNOWLEDGMENTS

Creation of this work was made possible in part by an Artist Trust Grants for Artist Projects (GAP) award. Find out more at www.artisttrust.org.

The author gratefully acknowledges the following publications in which the following poems first appeared:

Cascade: Journal of the Washington Poets Association, "Sonnet for the Three of Cups, Reversed"

Many Trails to the Summit anthology, Rose Alley Press, "Sonnet for The Moon", "Sonnet for The Star"

Snow Monkey, "Divination", "Sonnet for The Fool"

TABLE OF CONTENTS

THE SITUATION & WHAT CROSSES IT

Divination

Three sparrows on a wire.
No weighty portent, this.
I search mosquito bites, my mumped-up face
for signs. Last year, before
our trouble started, you said:
Scarlet parrots with emerald eyes
escaped from the pet shop, perhaps,
an aviary at the zoo,
or the cynical widow's window box,
feral now, unfurled
upon the city's twilit shoulders.
Raucous cries commute their gorgeous warning.
But now the only sound to heed, the folding
of road maps in my lap. Listen:
the refolding.

THE QUERENTS

Sonnet for the Three of Cups

We're in our cups & telling fish stories
that are, in fact, about our fish. Our fish
reveal our penchant for soliloquies:
a goldfish swims in a martini glass;

he grows & grows until he graduates
to bathtub. *Full of gin*, you say & raise
your glass. On & on the anecdotes
pour out. A fog of tonic, cabarets.

We drive ourselves to drink. I'd say *like fish*,
except that fish don't swallow water. Gulps
are merely their red herring. Osmosis
the only way to plumb the depths or cross the Alps.

My friend, you are my kind, my tribe, a shot
of favorite whiskey, fishing net, my knot.

Sonnet for the Ten of Wands, Reversed

One must imagine Sisyphus happy.
—Albert Camus

Yes, leave me at the mountain's foot! Absurd
to think that you won't find a burden
of your own. Look there—the carrion birds
forever beak & pluck & keen. Kind wardens

who sing a lullaby of blood & rust
each night. I love the colors of the earth;
admit that martyrdom's a kind of lust.
Admit you feel it, too. Struggle itself

enough to fill the heart. If life is work,
it's also motion, cleverness, a game
of chance. Let's call it paper, scissors, rock.
I'll tell you a secret: there was one time

the boulder came to rest atop the hill.
I nudged it so it rolled right back to hell.

Sonnet for La Mort (XIII)

> *Let be be finale of seem.*
> —Wallace Stevens,
> "The Emperor of Ice-Cream"

The king is trampled, reaped. The maiden feigns
& flutters, barely catches breath. Coxswain

calls *stroke & stroke* to cross the river Styx.
Those blushing cheeks mere *livor mortis*: pricks

her finger, falls asleep. Supine, toe-tagged,
so cocksure. Lovely fetish, bound & gagged

for calling *cuckoo*, calling over
& over to the other side. Rigor-

ously stiffens. An art of daily
death only means it's getting easier.

Don't believe it? Be a man & lift the sheet.
Those sharp & brassy horns are just *petite*

metaphors for tongue or blade or wife.
Watch what she is & does—undone—for life.

Sonnet for the Four of Swords

Let us reassure you: this is not
a time of death. We call it *writer's block*
or *hibernation*. We are somnolent,
hypnotized by the swinging watch: tick-tock

tick-tock. We'd like to strap our armor on
& slay the dragon, but the hours slip
away. Like sand or damselflies, the dawn's
glow. We're tired of such tired tropes.

You're tired too. Mix *stupor* with *attack*
& join us, narcoleptic. You'd rather
see your navel, button-fly, dental plaque
between these sheets & we would rather

write them. When we dream, we dream the sun
illuminates the stained glass crimson.

Sonnet for the Nine of Cups

Be careful what you wish for. That old saw!
A wish is more than a morality
tale, warning, plot device, unwritten law
of greed & consequences. Reality

is not a genie in a lamp. I have
a tumbler full of wine. Let's drink to
ridiculous requests: sons misbehave,
transform to ravens. Children misconstrued

as hedgehogs, hazel nuts, or sprigs of myrtle.
Extremely literal perversions
like corpses animating: *de rigueur,*
of course. Raise your cup & pick your poison:

twilight's first star, deep well, or dandelion.
Little fork of bone once made for flight, now broken.

Sonnet for the Nine of Pentacles, Reversed

The bird & cage, they both were hers. Her knees,
the garden, digging up bulbs. As if the bird
were shoulders & a mane. As if quarry
or mine. Mind, the early warning. Send word

of wind that twists a red shirt on the line.
A hooded thing, the heart. She cannot love
her jesses or anklets. Among her vines
& vineyards, searches for a leather glove.

The falconer is frightening the fowl
to make them rise. A red-tailed hawk will seize
her birdy body & she grieves for all
that die in her backyard. Bad luck in threes:

she is the shirt, the heart, the weapon.
A bird is on the branch. It is a lion.

Sonnet for the Knight of Cups

I remember now: I used to have a fish
held in a golden cup. She'd speak to me
of dream-things: fronds; a crystal butter dish;
bright plumage of a parrot. Blues & greens

remind me of the sea. I had a fish
but now I ride this horse along the shore.
I broke a spell; out fell a girl with wheyish
skin. I left her, which I am sorry for

as she was fair & kind to me. A fish
stitched on my sleeve in crimson yarn is all
I have. The color red a rash; an itch;
a too-tight boot; a roan mare births a foal.

Imagine my fish: rosy, flushed, offstage.
She is a messenger. In fact, the message.

Sonnet for The Fool (0)

I am the *me* in mine own story:
one step away from cliff, a handkerchief
hung on a stick. Stray dog, I'm you. You're me,
so deeply leap, your whiskers so! Try this:
deal six cards to the dog. *Le chien*, the kitty,
a face-down pile: the *valet, cavalier,*
the *dame & roi.* Don't forget *moi*, say me.
I'm your excuse, your guard against the way
that zero multiplies. As zero, I
rule no one yet I'm equal to the king.
No fooling, no u-turns. The joker's wild,
out of the game. Talk about trick-making!
I count me in & on each hand, unspoken
triumph: never taking, never taken.

Sonnet for the Two of Pentacles, Reversed

It started as a banal act. Sideshow
huckster tossing objects on the midway.
Rubber balls, apples, & *diabolos*
in common patterns like reverse cascade.

One day, I told my feeder, *Add some danger.*
Like knives, flaming torches, chainsaws. The crowd
was rabid. Ravenous. I took on more:
a golden fish, canary, mushroom cloud,

& babies! At least a dozen babies
now fly in arcs above. They are not mine,
but they belong to me. A galaxy
of *round* surrounding us. The bottom line

is that Atlas had it easy. Just one earth!
Next time, try juggling the universe.

Sonnet for the Six of Cups, Reversed

But then, one day, a sudden sprouting all
around her. Rather, avalanche. Tsunami
of babies. Babies! In a closet full
of coats, a dozen paper origami

babies peek from pockets. O, she sees them!
On subway cars, behind the polish of
the silver knives, beneath the tailored hems
of ladies at the bar. *I need kid gloves,*

she thinks, & thinks it started with her cry
of warning. *Wolf*, she knows, is not a drill
but no one listens. *Mother May I?*
is but a koan & snarled in yarn, cat's cradle.

No, you can't do that. You may instead
take forty baby steps. Forward, backward.

THE CELTIC CROSS (I)

Sonnet for Temperance (XIV)

Consider *temper*: bittered sling, we've slung
our insults, rendered our old-fashioned hearts
both stout & bold. The same time muddled, hung-
-on & -over. My *bon vivant*—stalwart

companion slugging punches, sours, flips—
I'll tell you a story. Most of it's false
but you've knocked back a dozen glasses
& you'll likely swallow anything else.

So listen up: there's both wrath, creation.
The steel is heated, quenched. Last night we sat
half in the gutter near the Greyhound station.
Tonight, we're dry & in our cups, winking at

Archangel Ariel, who's tending bar.
He wields the shaker, lights our drinks on fire.

Sonnet for the Three of Cups, Reversed

> *The name of the star is Wormwood. A third of*
> *the waters turned bitter, and many people*
> *died from the waters that had become bitter.*
> —Revelation 8:11

If tall, if grooved. If silver-green. If green,
then tonic, febrifuge. All-purpose patent
remedy for our bellyaches & spleen.
Bewitching hour's not what we thought: *l'heure verte*
degenerates, makes werewolves of our moods.
Good Doctor Ordinaire prescribes three sweet
cubes lined up on tiny slotted spoons.
Cold-water blossoms milky-white: *petite
louche*, our proof that three-to-one dilution
clouds the mind. Sugar, I don't need your mouth-
feel now: how thick, how mad. Hallucination
in a *demi-tasse*, devil-in-a-glass: both
of us starving-green, green flame, green seedling star
anise green-felled by gravity, gone far.

Sonnet for The Emperor, Reversed (IV)

"If all Greeks are philosophers," you said,
"it follows that we are not Greeks." "It's true,"
I said, "that A is B." All men are dead,
which is to say we're mortal. Olives' ooze

& ouzo: not our style. "Olive juice, too,"
you said & took my hand. Syllogism
slipped once again to solipsism. You...
Ellipsis & elliptical, —isms

will make their points then fade away & we
are more like circus geeks, full of beak
& feather, baleful eye & crop. Peck-
ing order, pecker. If *you* are *me*,

all *me* is *meat*. We then conclude:
wishbone, drumstick, cockfight.

Sonnet for The Star (XVII)

This day before dawn I ascended a hill and look'd
at the crowded heaven and I said to my spirit,
When we become the enfolders of those orbs, and
the pleasure and knowledge of everything in
them, shall we be fill'd and satisfied then?
—Walt Whitman

If kneeling on the ground, half-stepping in
the creek to fill these jugs, makes me bullish,
can you bear it? As it happens, we've been
camping before. It makes us churlish:
we argue about who should fetch & who
should carry; whether you should spark the fire
or be the one to tend it. We make do,
because the greedy flames will never tire
& sticks grow scarce. The brightest star tonight
seems far, flung off: Orion's undone belt.
He hunts a hot blue hart, his line-of-sight
unbent. I wonder if you've ever felt
like seven lovely ladies followed by
a cruel pursuer: draw, release, bull's eye.

Sonnet for The Moon (XVIII)

Do not look through the pinhole at the sun,
you say, & hold the card, while I remark
that you didn't use a pin to poke it. One
plus eight is nine, but I would argue hard
for two, or seven, purely out of spite.
Our eclipse season's back again. Repeat
after you: *penumbra, umbra,* pearly-white
curl, *solar corona.* But not me.
I'm *annular aura,* negative shadow,
a ring-around-the-rose at maximum
phase. My pockets full of *why & how,*
but all I really want to do is hum
the soundtrack to my life. It's *Claire de Lune.*
You think you're looking at the sun, but it's the moon.

Sonnet for the Seven of Wands

That spring, the branches filled with pallid pink.
The gutters choked with white. Petals, of course,
but I thought: *snow*. And poured another drink.
"March," you said, like you were giving orders

to someone who would listen. Our cat went mad
at all the twilit windows, wanting out
or wanting *want*. "He wants to hunt," you said,
"To gift a gutted rodent." Well, no doubt

you were referring to yourself instead.
If you're a tom, then I'm your molly. Droll,
we think, until it's not. Until we're dead
or scooped up in the catcher's net. Parole

or anesthesia? It won't be easy, *will*
the only everything left. Mountain. Molehill.

Sonnet for the Queen of Wands

I'm dark, but not black-hearted. Call it *self*
or *solid*. Cat-a-mountain, anarchist,
the cat's meow. I howl; I cross your path.
You cross yourself & mutter *egotist*

but talk is cheap. Bewitched & -witching,
you find me more familiar than your face
reflected in my eye. I'm walking
two-legged on & off the plank. Worst-case

scenario? The ship will sink, while I
enjoy a shot of vodka, game of chess.
A Molotov cocktail, my Cheshire smile,
& sabotage is nothing more than this:

I pour the booze then light 'em up & toss.
Call it using a little black cat on the boss.

Sonnet for the King of Cups

A sudden nose bleed, after yet another
argument about the cat. It is just
like in the movies: small, unnoticed
trickle—lightly wiped—that goes a-gusher.
It takes an hour to clot & so I'm sure
that I'm a *femme fatale*, a leggy actress
who plays George Clooney's wife. I'm diagnosed:
leukemia or rare brain tumor,

which makes George Clooney sad. He watches me
with haunted eyes for the rest of our short life
together. He makes amends & I forgive
him. Nick of time. But I am not George Clooney's
wife. I'm yours. You tilt my head, bring ice
with lime & gin. You say, "I think you'll live."

Sonnet for the King of Wands, Reversed

A nemesis is never born of void
or vacuum. Rivals do not simply fall
upon us like a starving wolf. I am destroyed,
unmasked by my own hand. The mask a caul.

Desire must be dissected. *Ardor?*
Call it lust or electricity, a flame
that sputters in the windy corridor
that is my yellowed heart. Revulsion, shame

at what I've wrought & wrung. A fever
rages in me. The lab is torched, a scorched
earth cries out: *revenge.* Creator, master?
These words are merely sewn together, stitched

& stretched across what I see in the mirror:
my nemesis & my beloved monster.

Sonnet for the Queen of Cups, Reversed

At the end of it, I'm left alone
to sit & stare at this closed cup. It looks
ridiculous, ornate: a golden crown.
Ironic. Emptied of both the milk

of human kindness & direst cruelty,
it's still of use. I have some trouble
sleeping. Cups can be filled with whiskey
or wine. Wine may be spilled. Indelible

stains on the linoleum, my nightgown,
the white shag rug. As if any woman
who had a husband would end face down
with dishpan hands, unsexed, hung-over &

somnambulist. As if marriage was a dream.
A girl, lost in a wicked wood. Her screams.

THE CELTIC CROSS (II)

The Tarot Card Sonnets Lose Their Luster

One day, the cards no longer fascinate
her. Bored, she shuffles the deck again &
again. *It's not hard to articulate,*
she thinks. *You deal yourself a hand*

but you can't play patience, call it solitaire,
with pentacles & wands. Better to invest
her time in the casino, a love affair
with hearts & clubs. Cardiac arrest,

Neanderthal one-liners. Better than
fourteen. A sonnet's a machine, a form-
ula, deep heartbreak on installment plan.
Her initial vision: a violent storm

of divination. The end result?
Two-beat phrases written only by default.

Sonnet for the Eight of Pentacles

A sonnet is a building-block, a room,
a brick, a landscape in a boxy frame.
Our history feels heavy, locked. Presume
failure. Call it *prison, coffin, card game.*

A deck with spades & diamonds. Only luck
if iambs scan correctly. We're counting
& re-counting, scratching shallow hatch marks
on the wall. A method of accounting

for all the years we've lost. Inadequate,
we stack the boxes, nail the lids on tight.
Bury them deep, or hang them with magnets
on the refrigerator door. *Rewrite*

the only writing left. Better to read
out in the sunny garden, among the weeds.

The Trouble is There is No Trouble

She's never seen a ghost except inside
her troubled heart. Pours a drink (a double)
& wonders if it will be Jekyll or Hyde
that shows his face tonight. She's unable

to predict, although she reads the cards
with care. She never likes what she sees—
cups filled with fish or coins—& disregards
the warnings. There are, of course, no guarantees

except for the paradox that statement
contains. Like *never say never.* James Bond
switched from martinis to an advertisement
for Heineken & she's considered blonde

in New England, but not in California.
A human life amounts to euthanasia.

Sonnet for the Nine of Pentacles, Reversed

The color of our childhood war is red.
But it's a cold one & we play at snow-
camps, prisons, spies. With *Sputnik* overhead,
we mouth exotic words like *Gulag, Mao,*

& *A-bomb.* Radiation makes monsters
of ants. Godzilla roars & burns a city;
eats everything whole. Practice hiding under
desks. *Stop & drop* our new vocabulary

for *blister, ulceration, bald.* Cover
your face & face away. Or so they say.
They say be hooded, watch, work harder.
An avalanche of snow signals decay.

We are Americans. We were. We are
the reaper's scythe. The hammer-blow of war.

The Problem

She tried to turn herself inside-out
& wear herself like a reversible
sweater. *That'll fix me up*, she thought,
I'll be someone new, someone reputable.

Trouble is, her ribs knock with soft music
like a xylophone & her tender red
heart *lub-dubs*, dumb animal. Quite a trick,
but it doesn't really solve much. Instead,

she's more herself than she ever was
before. More eviscerated, exposed,
more stitched & frayed. Graying, because
there's no disguising it. She's decomposed.

Or decomposing, anyway. So bring
the pickle jar, formaldehyde, o-ring.

History Does Not Repeat Itself

That would be a huge relief. Her life
makes carbon copies of itself, each one
blurrier, more smeared, frayed & graying. If
she squints, the inked-on words begin to run

together. A woman turning forty-
one drinks too much night after night & slips
on the wet street. Another martini
lets her forget herself & she forgets

with a vengeance. Loosens her tongue,
forgets exactly what she said, forgets
on purpose. Forgets that a glass rimmed
in bleary crimson lipstick

is no longer a seduction. Time used
to be. Now it's shaken & it's poured.

Sonnet for the Knight of Pentacles

If work is force across a distance, I
am in it for the long haul. *My pretty joule,*
you say. As if pack horse, as if plough.
Admittedly, I like routine: old-school

elbow grease or grindstone, nose-to-the.
My red caparison is beyond...well,
comparison. Harness & trappings.
I'm trapped but trot bejeweled, laurelled,

heralded & heralding the jackpot.
You think the harder you pull the lever
the better your chances. More often than not,
it dislocates your shoulder. I'll shoulder

the extra burden, lover. Take my bridle.
Reverse your boots. We're at a funeral.

Sonnet for the Three of Swords

It's hard to write of sorrow in this place
of daily gray & misting rain. Harder
still to account for the sublime: the grace
of terror spiked with awe. Here, we flounder

in damp & moldy apathy; we're passive-
aggressive. I used to keep a journal
to record it all in slanted cursive,
staggering sadnesses that signaled

nothing more than too much gin. The swords
that pierced my heart were, what? A fish,
a husband & a female friend. Minor chords
in a relatively major scale. Gothic

tales of storm & stress, a monster made?
More like swizzle sticks than bloody blades.

Jump Cut

She dreams in black & white. Correction:
dreams *of*. She wants to be a kerchiefed blonde
in a car, gazing at her reflection
in the side view mirror. Or beyond

herself, out into the flat-lined farmland.
The hot wind smells like hay. Her crimson
lips (we seem to know that they're stained red)
remind her of a bloody floor. She's on

the lam, pursued by cops or an ill-met
lover who wears a torn black suit. The next
frame shows her head turned right instead of left.
The audience is unsure, perplexed.

A closing couplet like a falling bone
or spinning satellite, obsidian.

Sonnet for the Seven of Pentacles

"I give up on the sonnet thing," she says & pours
another glass of wine.

Barbarism ends with cultivation of the olive & the vine.
The grapes incandescent, lit from inside. She thinks:
rain shadow, lee side.

Lately, all she sees is red. When she showers, hair dye
runs & stains the bath. There are textbook nosebleeds
with plenty of tissues & neck tilted back. She thinks:
Yes. Burgundy.

Iambs are fox-tracks.

Led astray, she uses filler phrases. Her heart lub-dubs
her blood around. She wants to say, "The articulation of
a complicated sense of place is called *terroir.*" What she
writes, of course, is: *of course; as if; because; in fact; you see.*

Leaving out the *i*, accidentally-on-purpose, she's left
with *terror.*

Notes on the Text

The Celtic Cross is a ten-card Tarot spread developed in the 1890s by a member or associate of the Golden Dawn. The spread was taught to first-level initiates of the Golden Dawn and was widely used after publication by Arthur E. Waite in his *Pictorial Key to the Tarot*.

Card 1: The main question on your mind, the situation

Card 2: A challenge within the situation, what crosses the situation

Card 3: The foundation of the question, subconscious issues

Card 4: The recent past

Card 5: Conscious goals, what you think you can achieve

Card 6: The near future

Card 7: What you are bringing to the situation

Card 8: How others affect the situation

Card 9: Your hopes and fears

Card 10: The outcome

"Sonnet for the Seven of Pentacles" is modeled after Bronwen Tate. The line *Barbarism ends with the cultivation of the olive & the vine* paraphrases the Greek historian Thucydides.

About the Author

Amy Schrader holds a B.A. in Molecular & Cell Biology and English Literature from the University of California at Berkeley, and an M.A. in English Literature from Boston University. She earned her M.F.A. in poetry from the University of Washington. She was a semi-finalist for the 2006 and 2007 "Discovery"/*The Nation* poetry contests, and a recipient of a 2008 GAP grant from Artist Trust.

Amy's poems have been published most recently in *The Monarch Review, Coconut Magazine, ILK, The Journal*, and *Willow Springs*. She received a work/study scholarship from the Vermont Studio Center in 1999, and also completed a residency at Hedgebrook in 2003. She was co-editor for *Borderlands: Texas Poetry Review* from 2001-2003, and Poetry Editor and co-publisher of *Cranky Literary Journal* from 2005-2007. Her reviews and interviews appear in *CutBank Reviews, Gently Read Literature, The International Examiner, Reading Local*, and other publications.

www.ingramcontent.com/pod-product-compliance
Lightning Source LLC
Chambersburg PA
CBHW022343040426
42449CB00006B/687